REAL LIFE

Thoughts & Quotes

Test Your Perspective, Purpose and Self Reflection

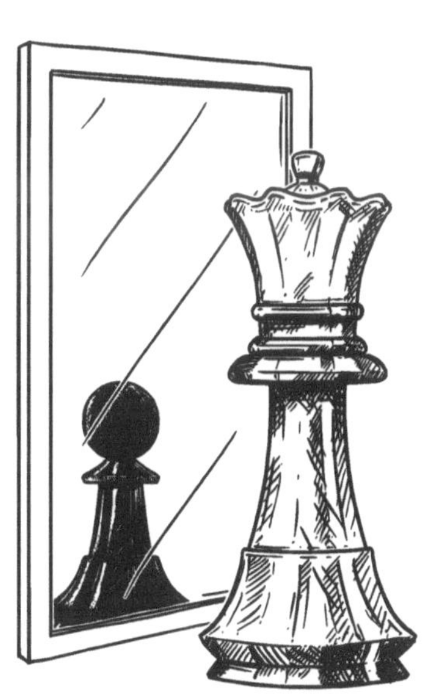

TONY SHINE

Smith & Knapp Publications

Hardcover ISBN: 979-8-9863204-0-3
Softcover ISBN: 979-8-9863204-1-0

This book is dedicated to my life coaches
Mom and Dad.
Thank you for always believing in me.

I want to thank my brilliant sister, Jennifer.
She supported me throughout this whole process
with her ideas, input and inspiration.

All illustrations are by the very talented
Belma Mehinagic
Thank you for bringing this book to life.

Print and eBook layout by
Robert Henry at Right Hand Publishing.

Why do quotes exist?

Because a lesson learned
is a lesson shared.

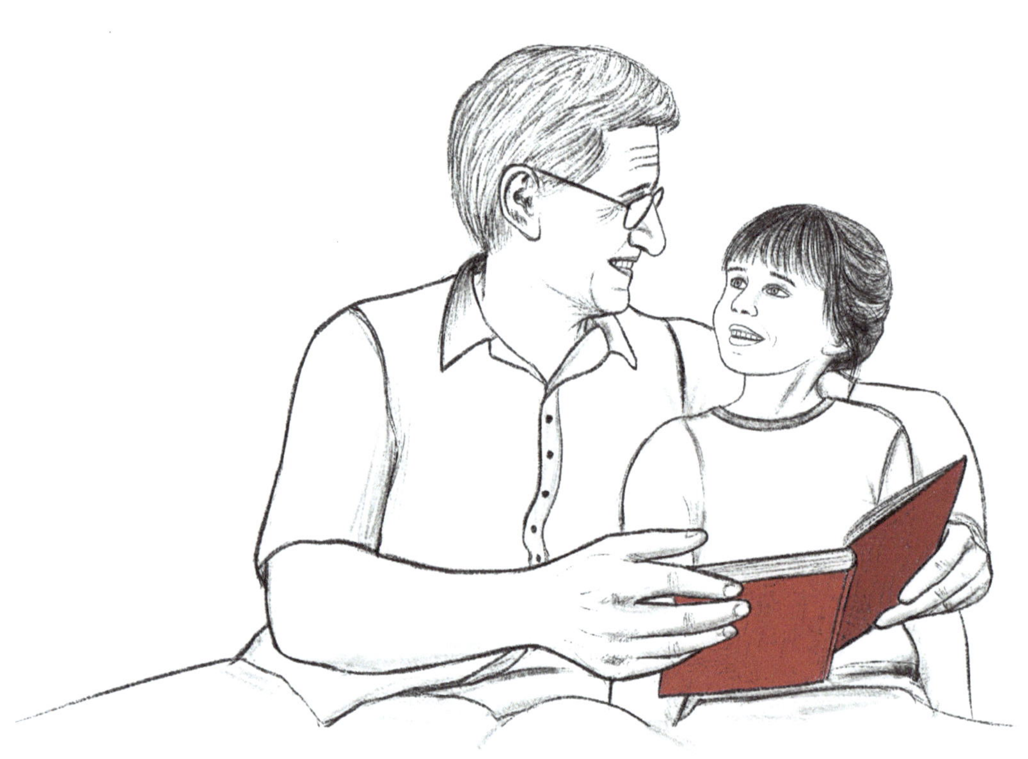

Those who resist change

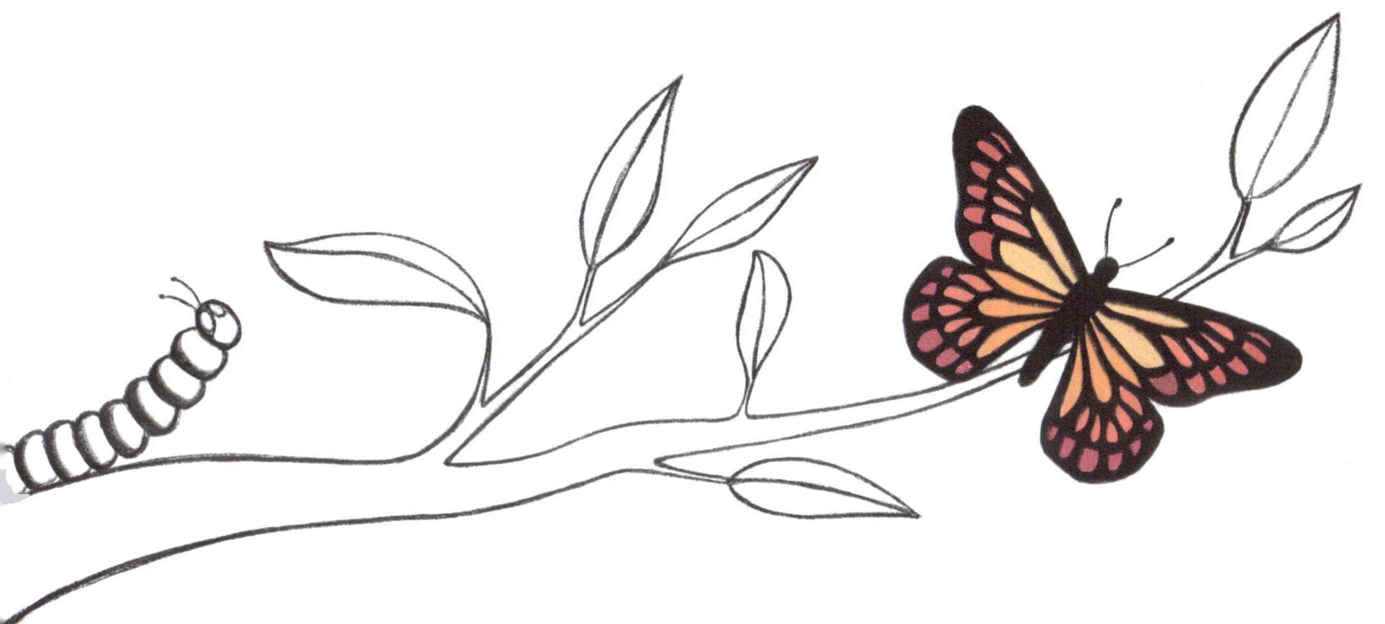

don't benefit from it.

You can't
stop someone
who has decided
to not give up.

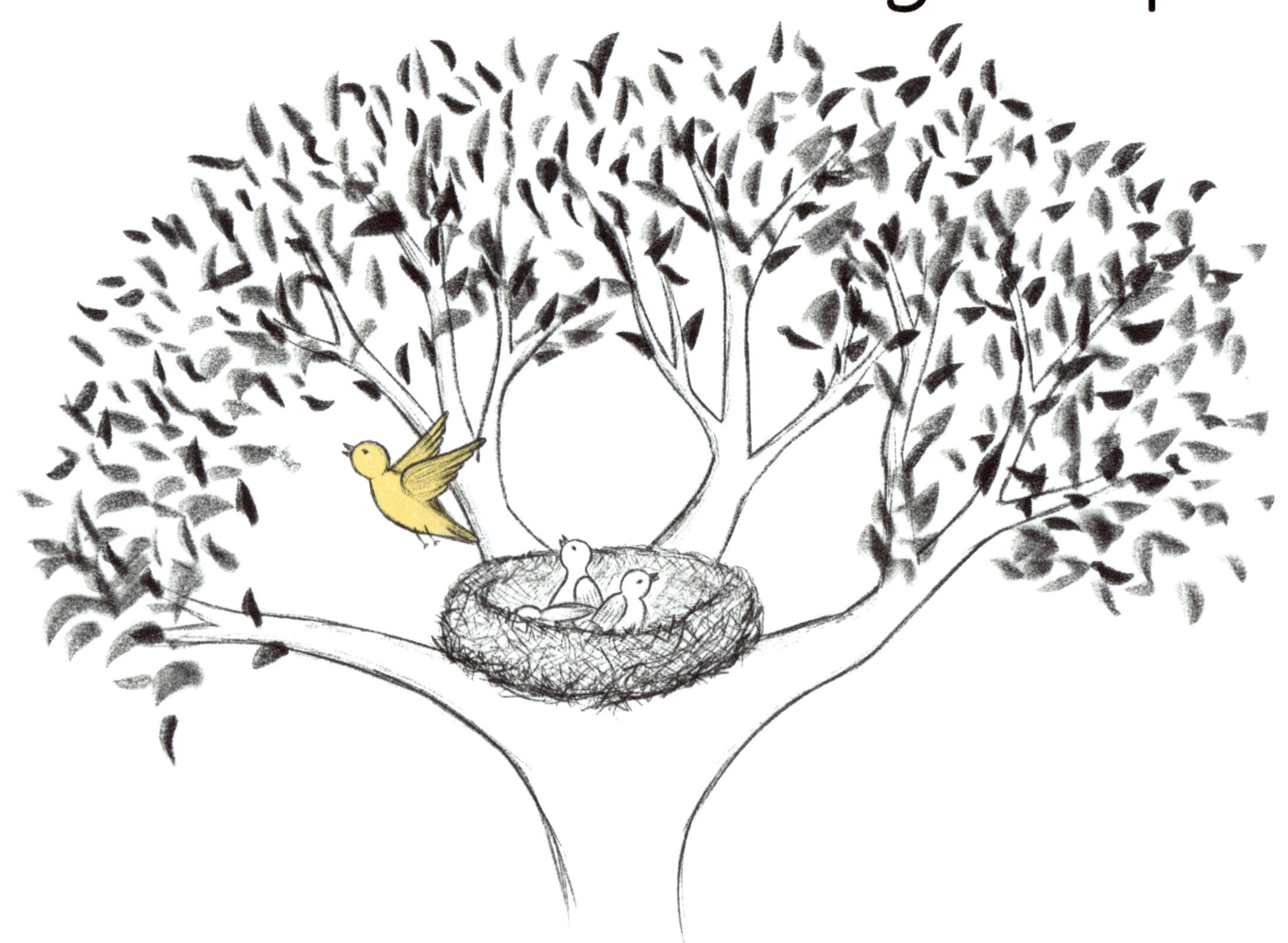

Let people be

FASCINATED

by you.

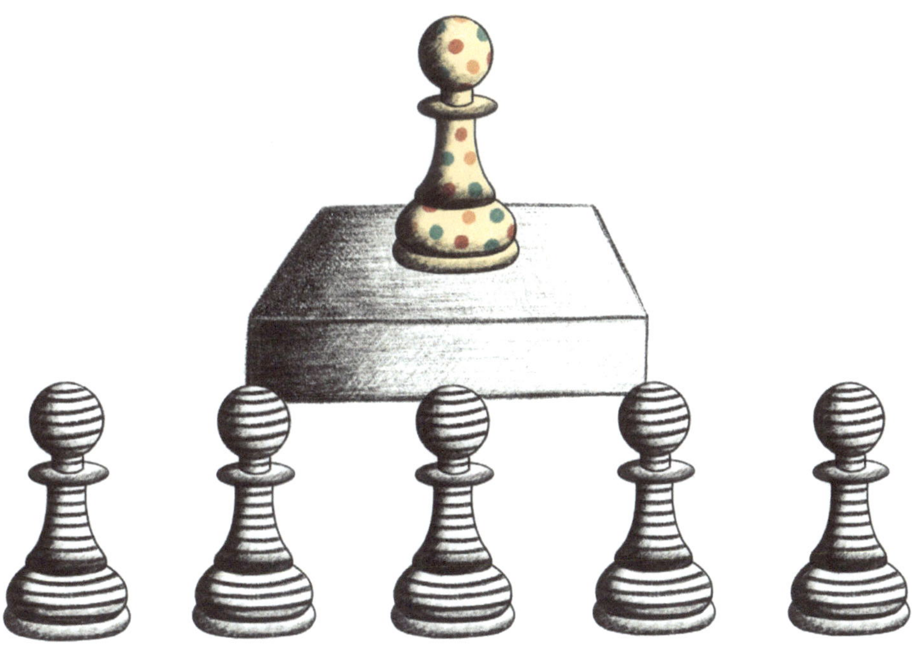

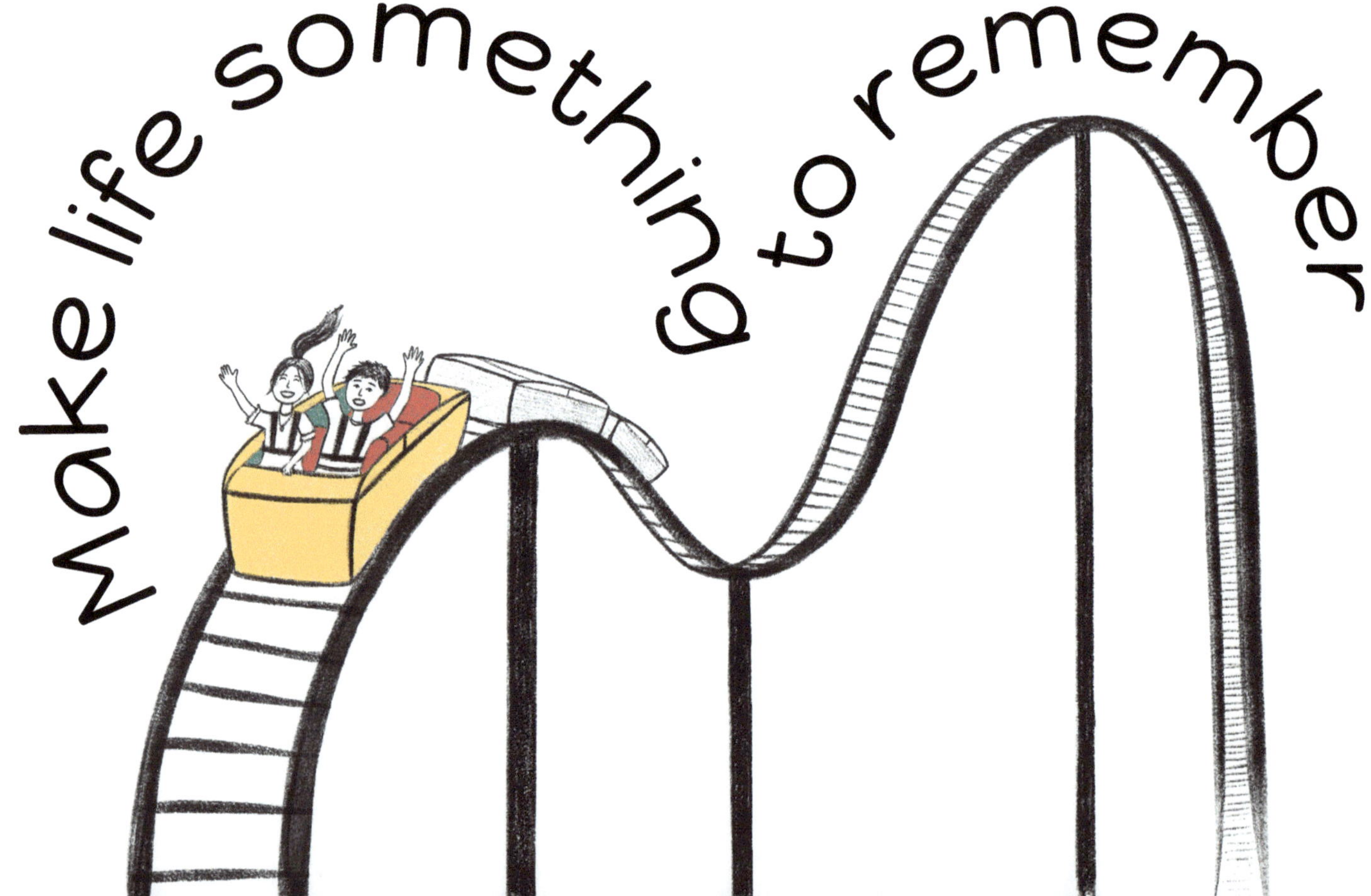

Make life something to remember

Overlooked and underrated. It's only a matter of time before the world catches on.

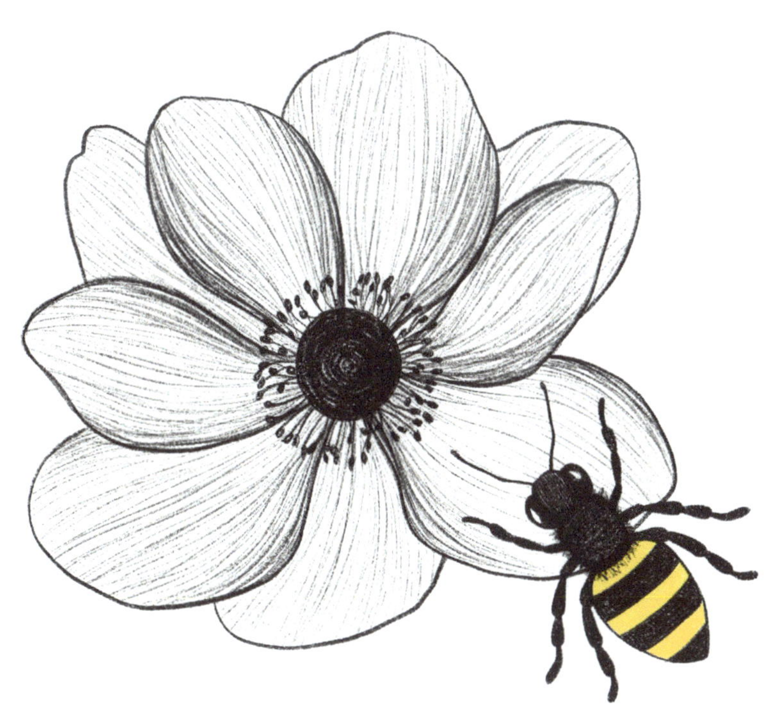

A good sentence is greater than the sum of its words.

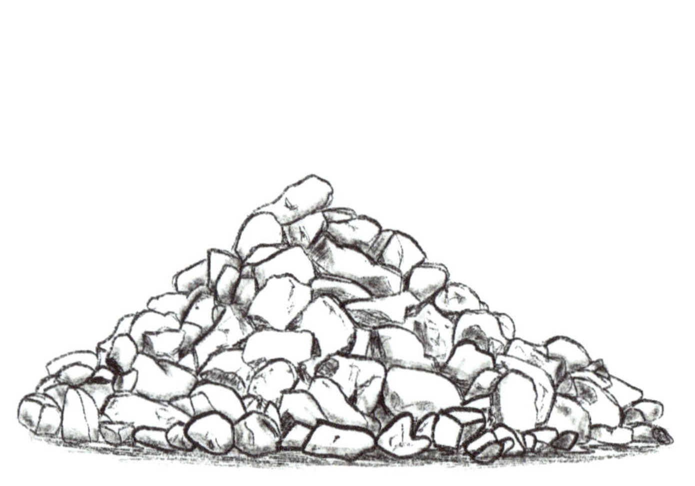

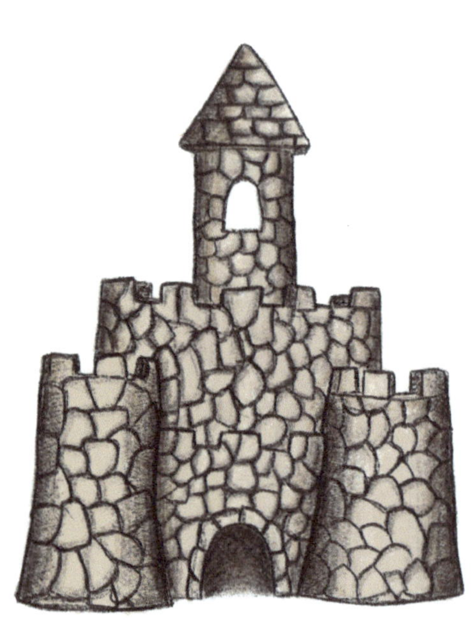

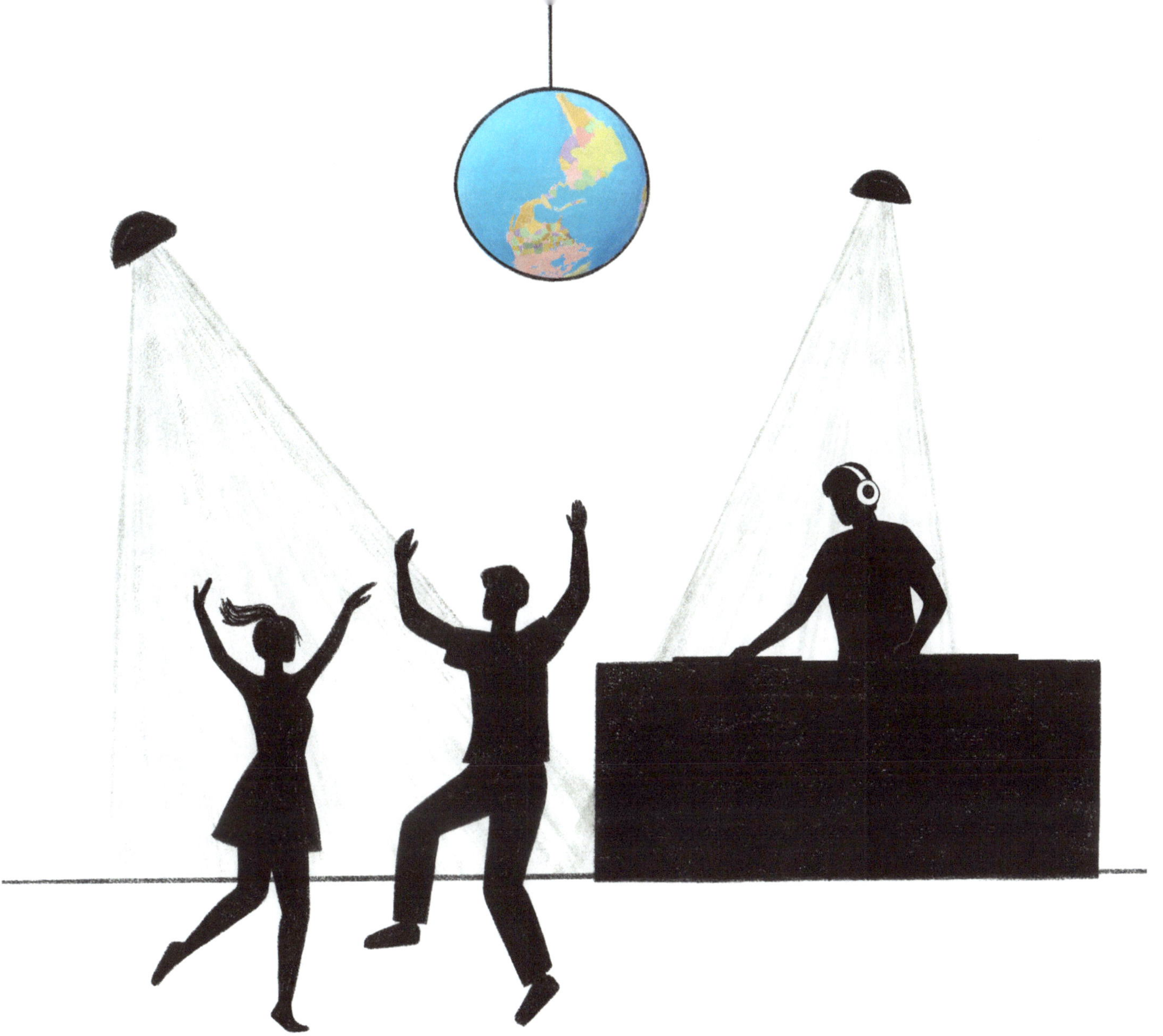

Enjoy the DJ even though he doesn't take requests.

People who get what they want tend to be the ones who know what they want.

Life will give you hints
like a gentle breeze.
For a moment, it spins the pinwheel.
You can see the dancing trees.
Enough for you to notice
but not everybody sees.

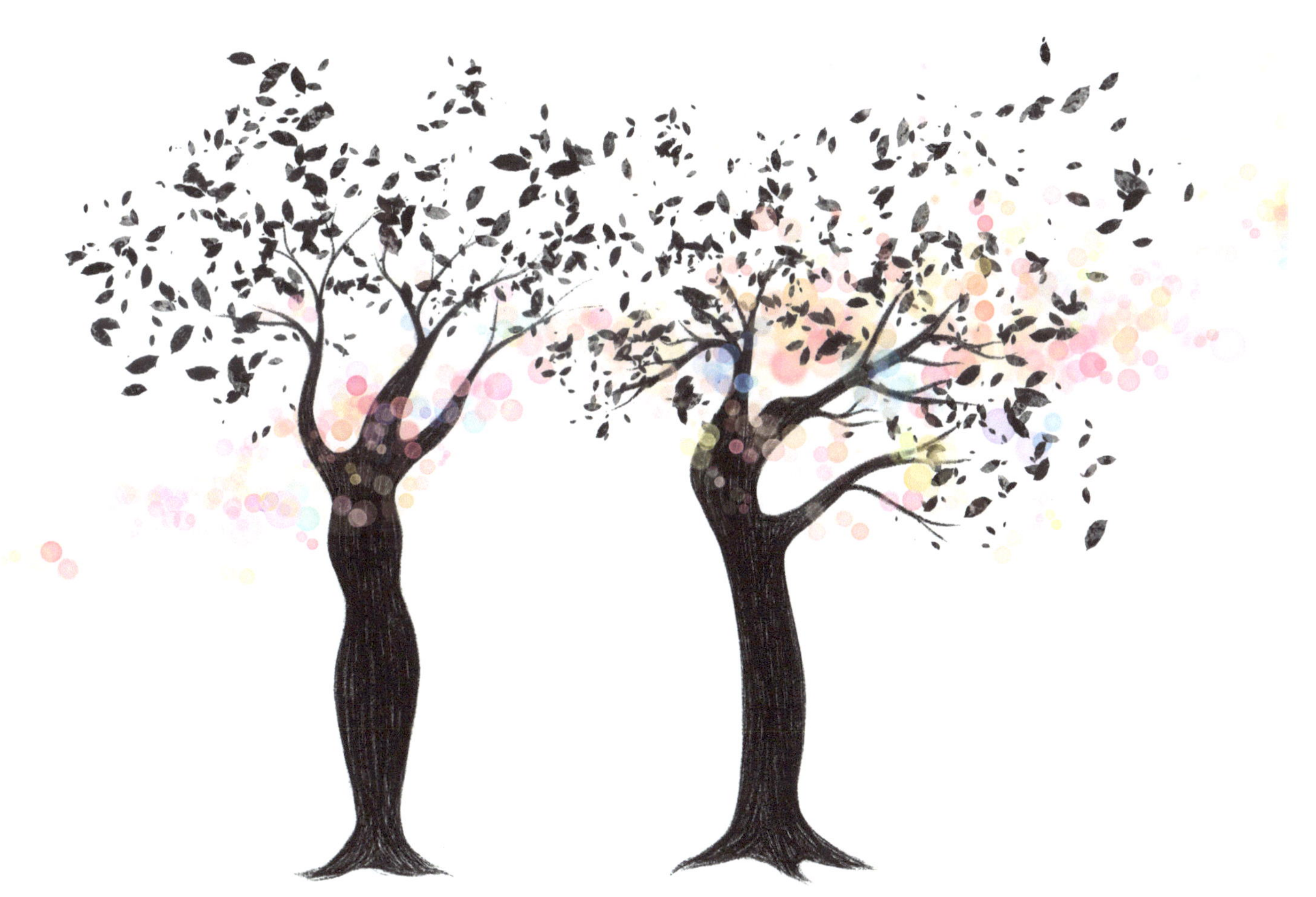

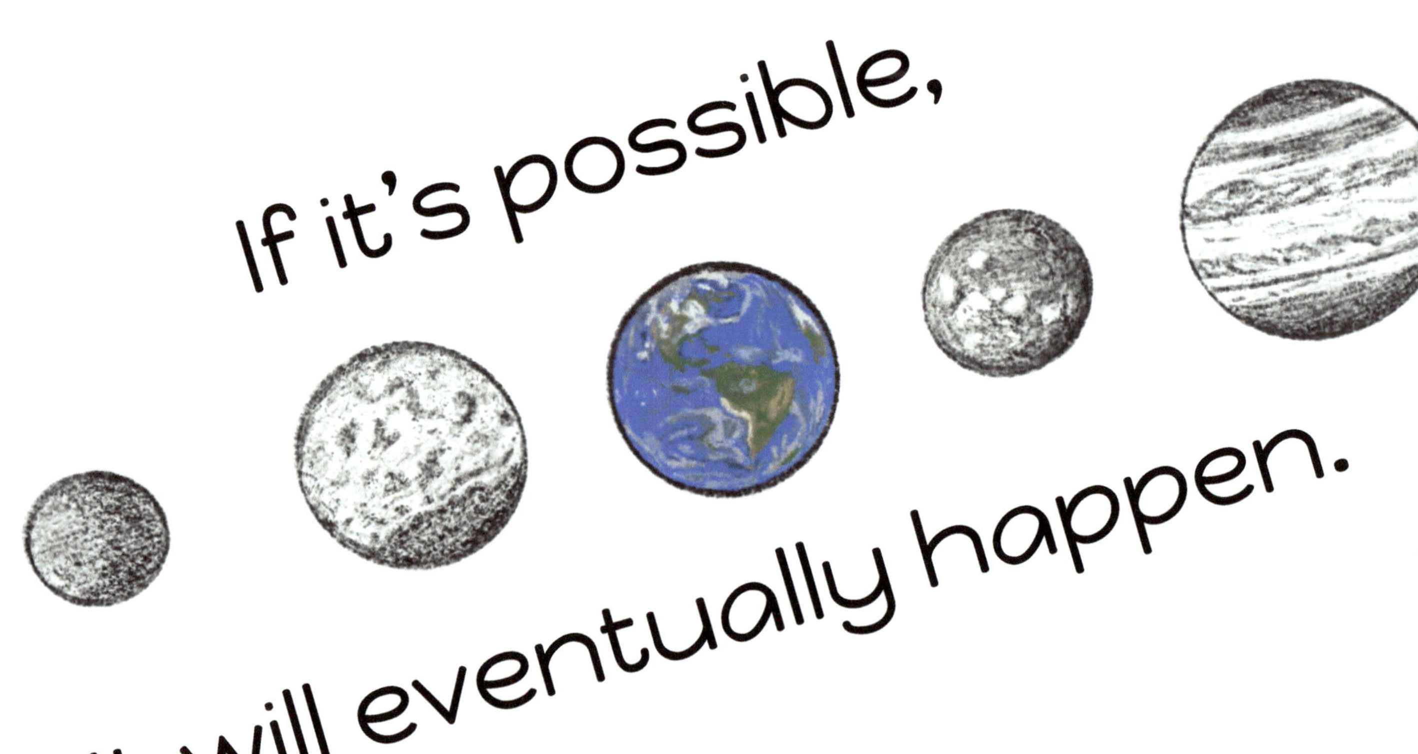

If it's possible,
it will eventually happen.

So, if you want something

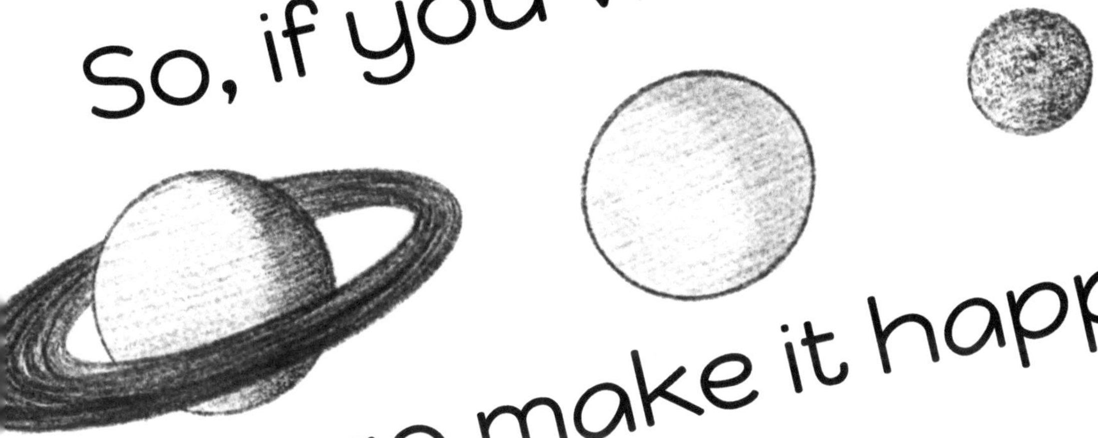

go make it happen.

Consider the consequences but follow the opportunities.

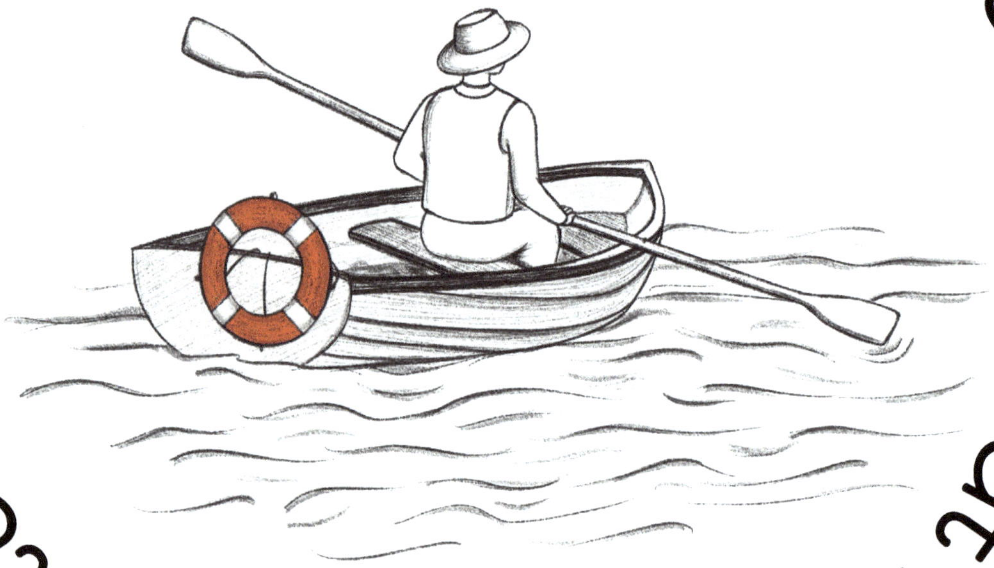

Life is what you're most **CURIOUS** about.

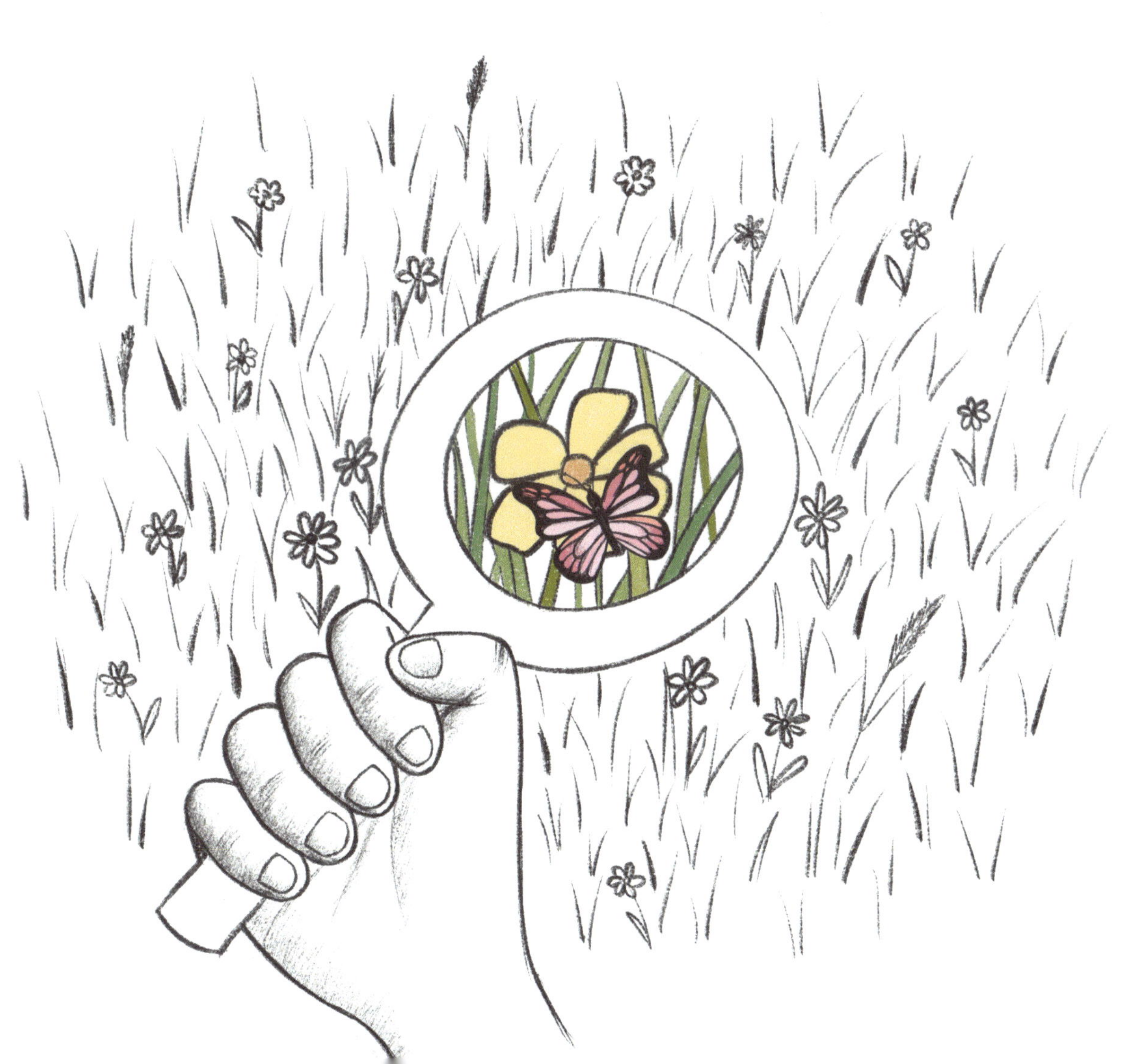

Face your problems.
Celebrate your successes.
Improve your craft.
Be grateful.

Love yourself.

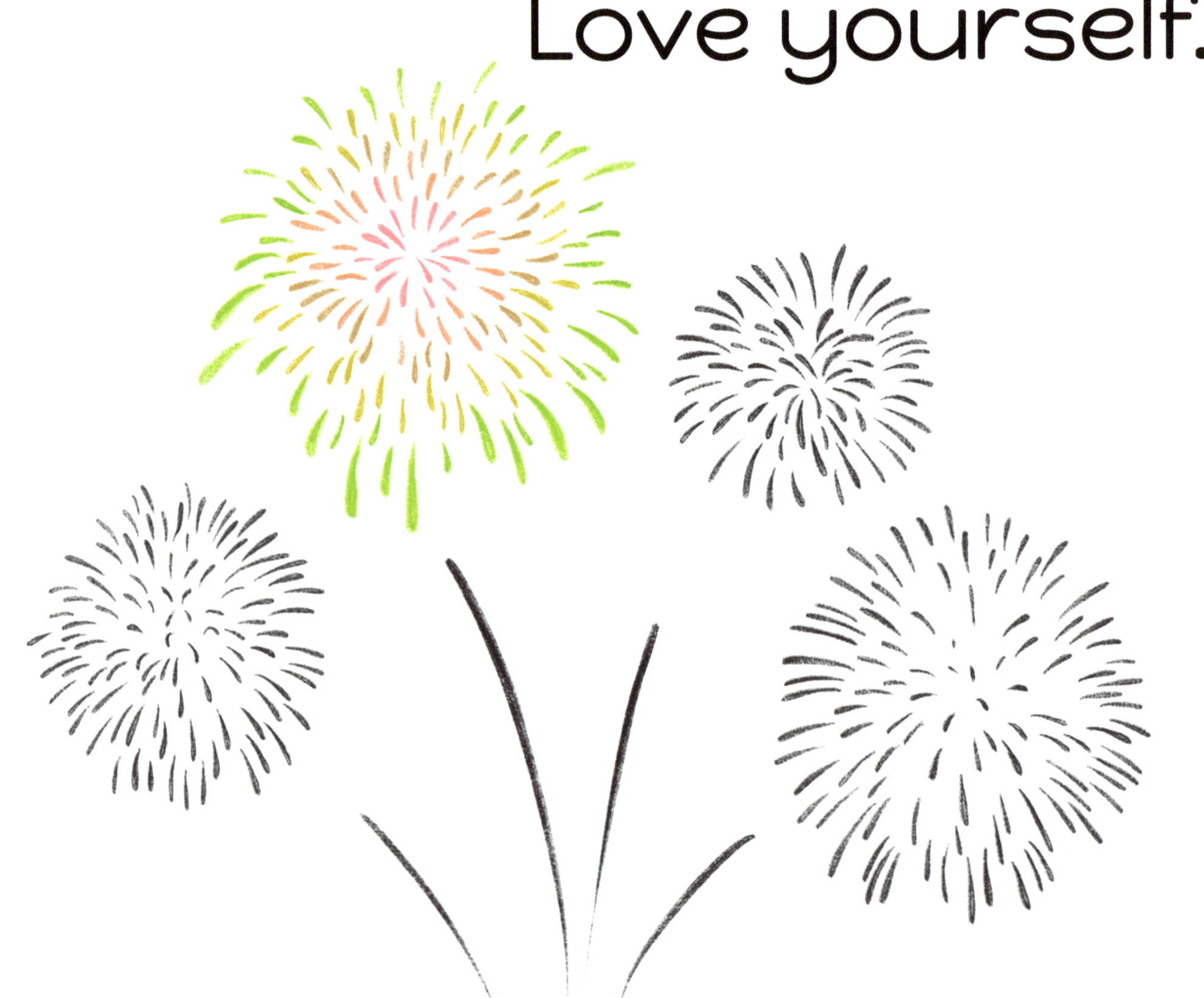

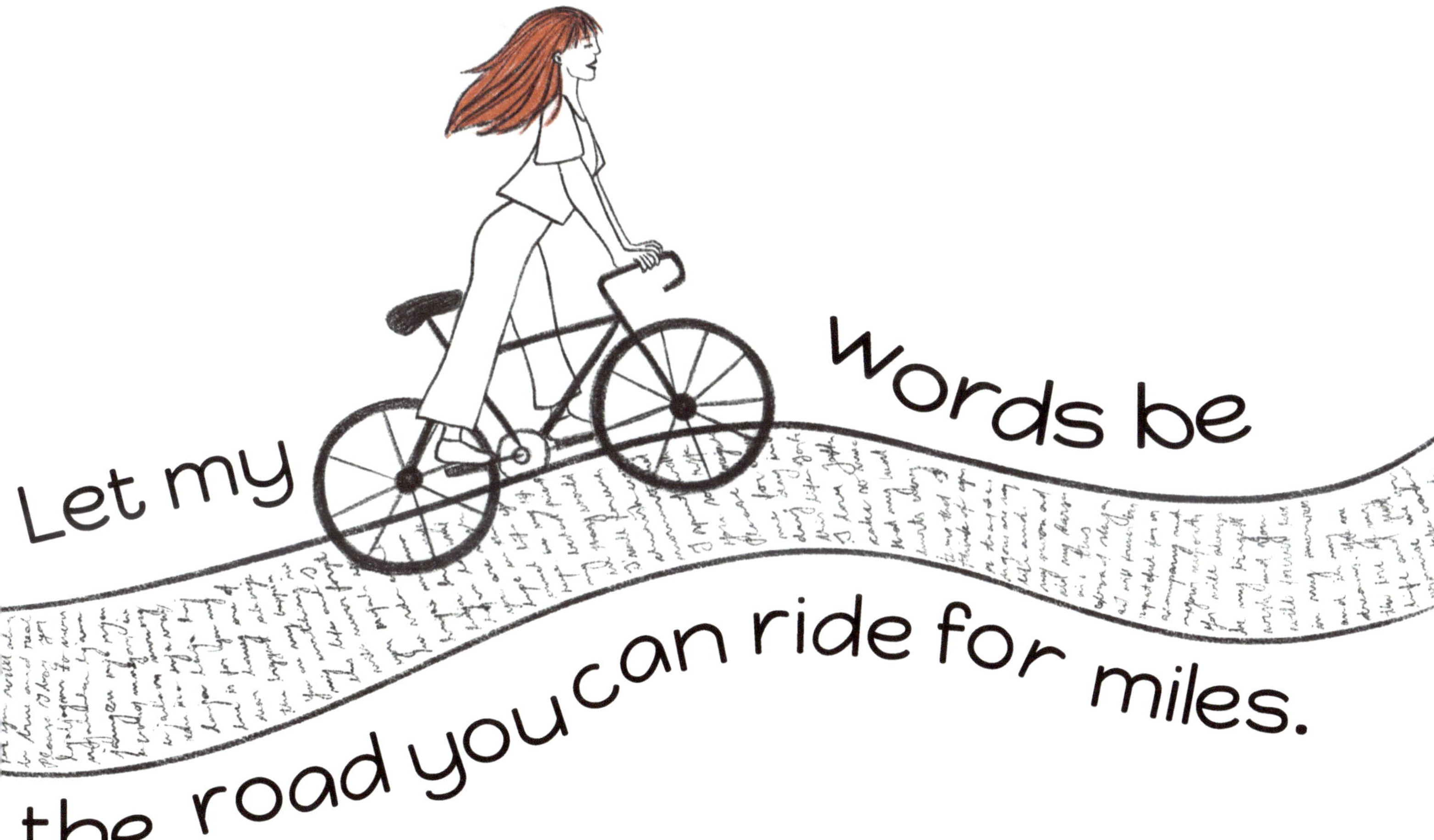

Let my
words be
the road you can ride for miles.

Even if
I have to
go my
whole
life just
believing,

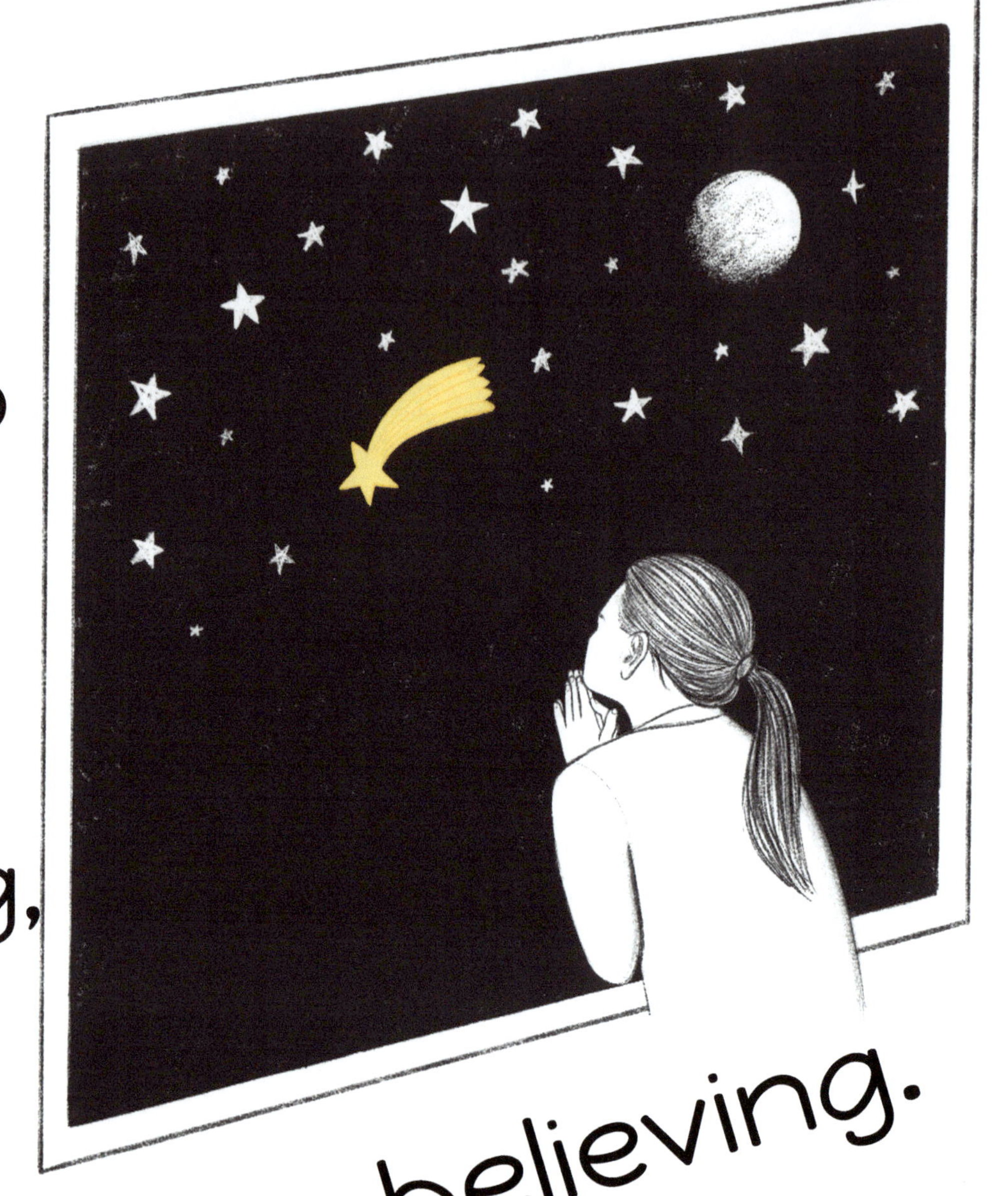

I will not stop believing.

Everyone exists
on purpose.

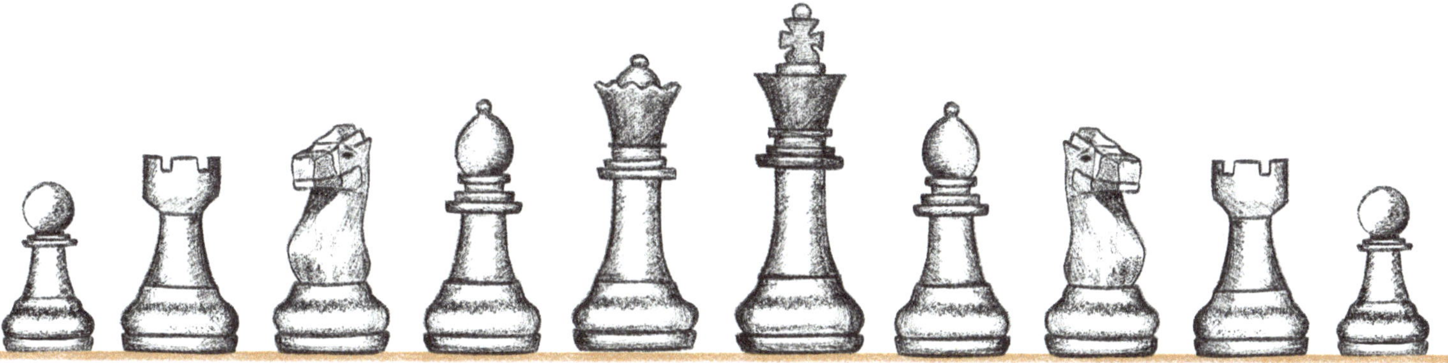

In a time of
so much knowledge
there's
something
about
having a
secret
that blinds
the world.

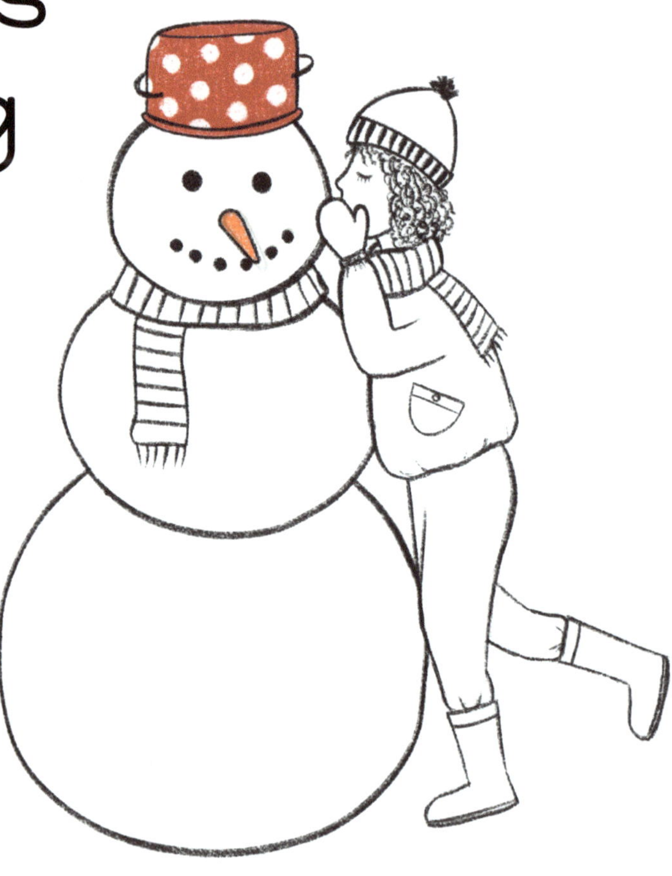

Life is shorter than you think
so _______ while you can.

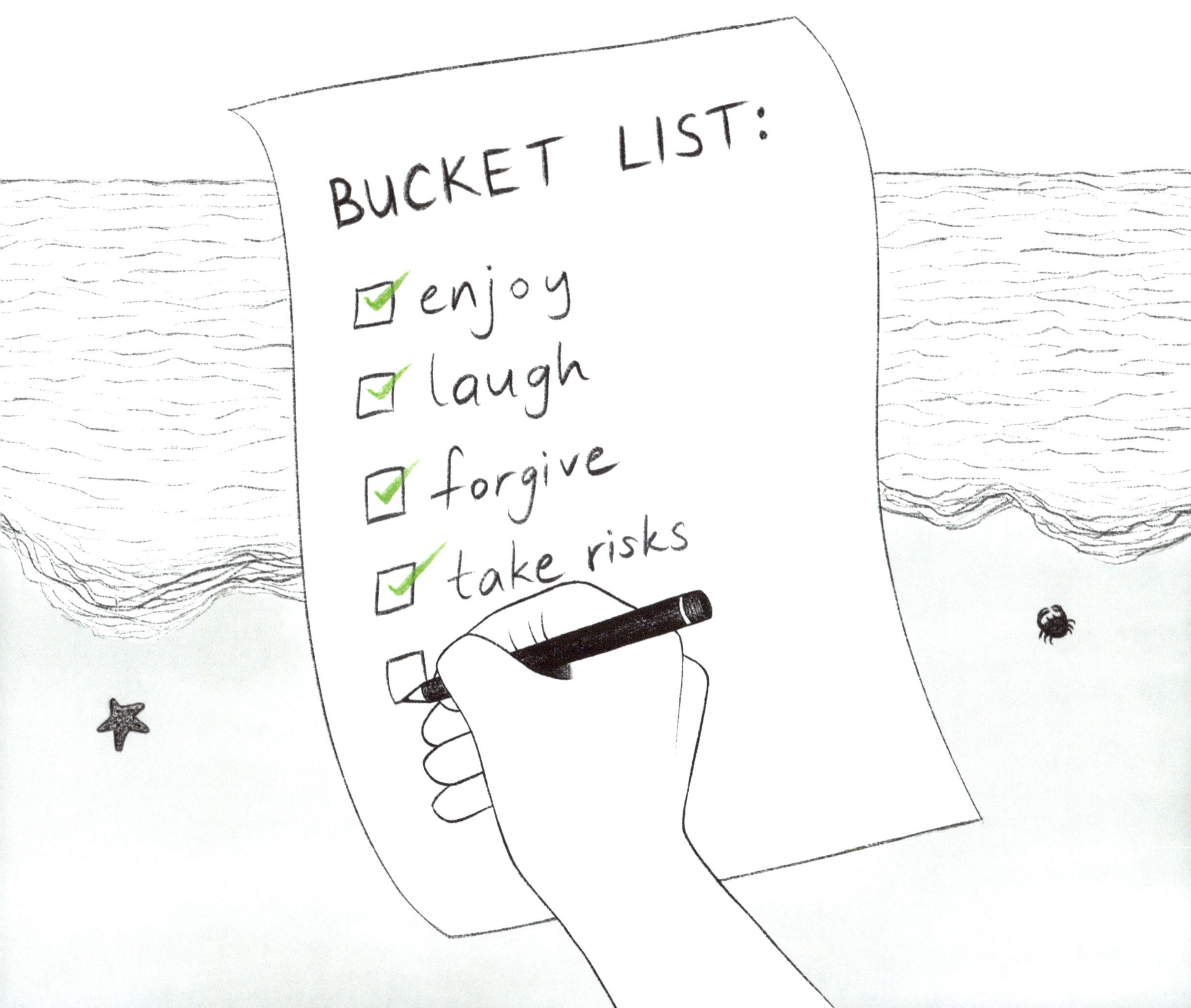

My eyes dance
around as I admire
the bouquet.
Wouldn't
it be nice to
be looked
at the
same
way?

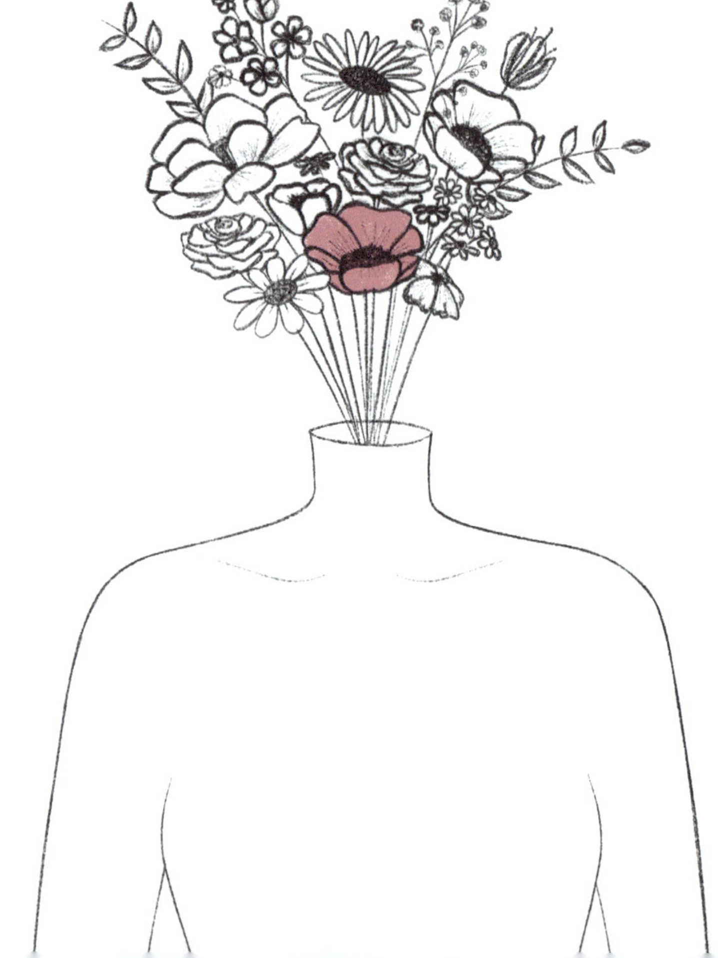

You already know the answers.

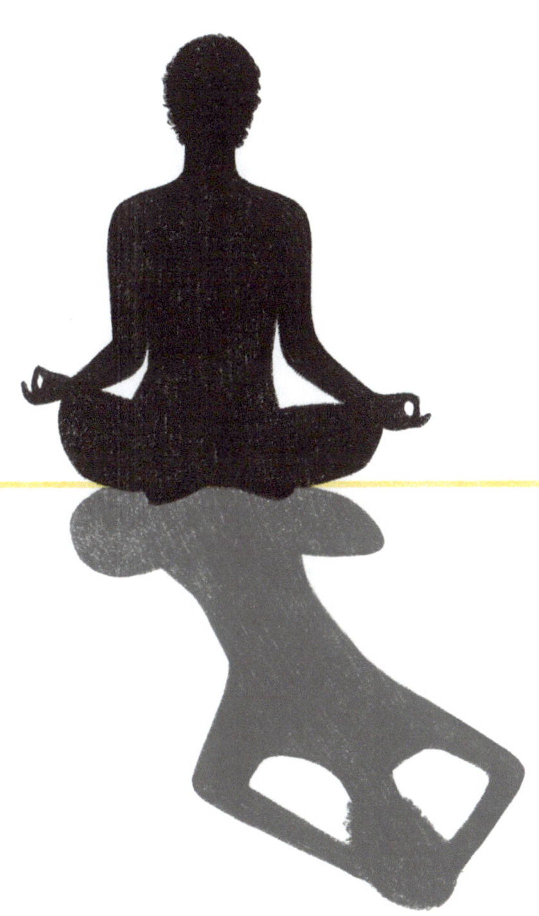

You just have to know that.

Don't strive to be popular.

Just know which people to invest in.

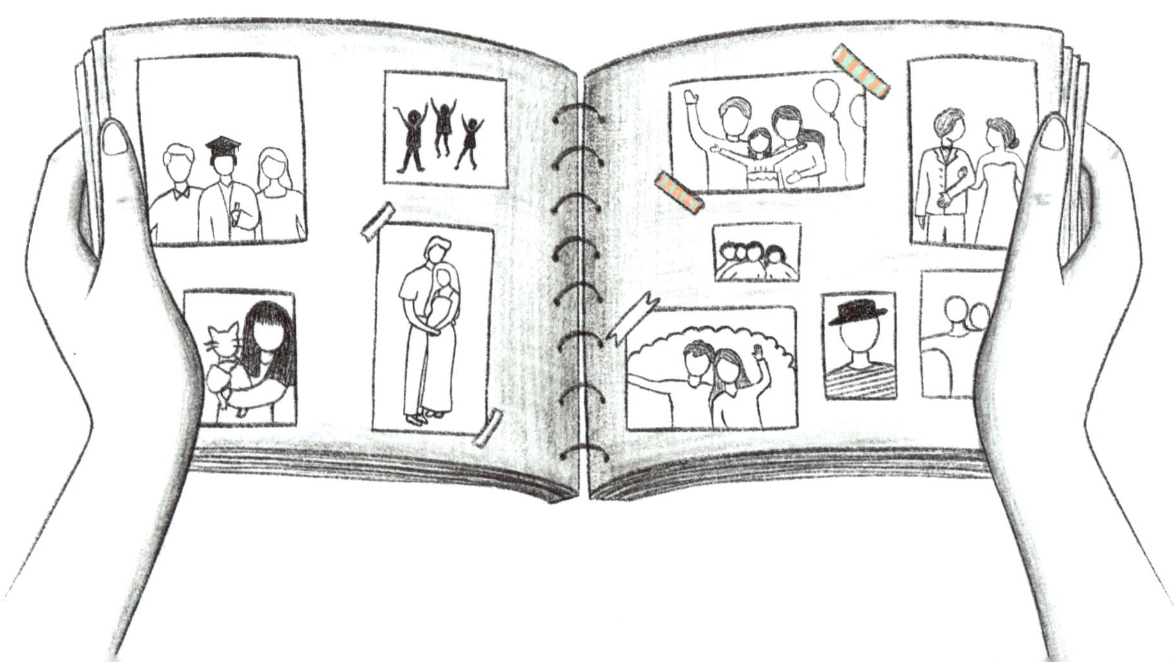

When there's certain cards
you don't play right away...

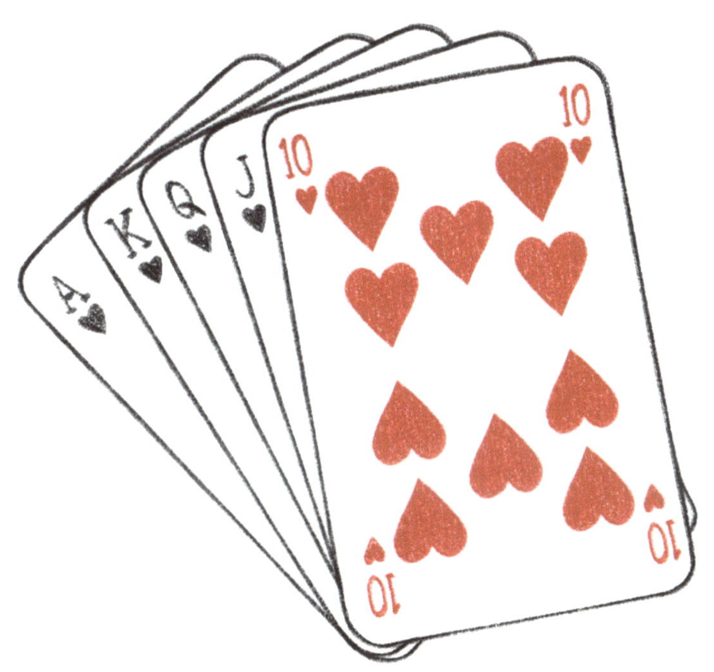

they appreciate over time.

You're not
the only one
who fought
for your life.

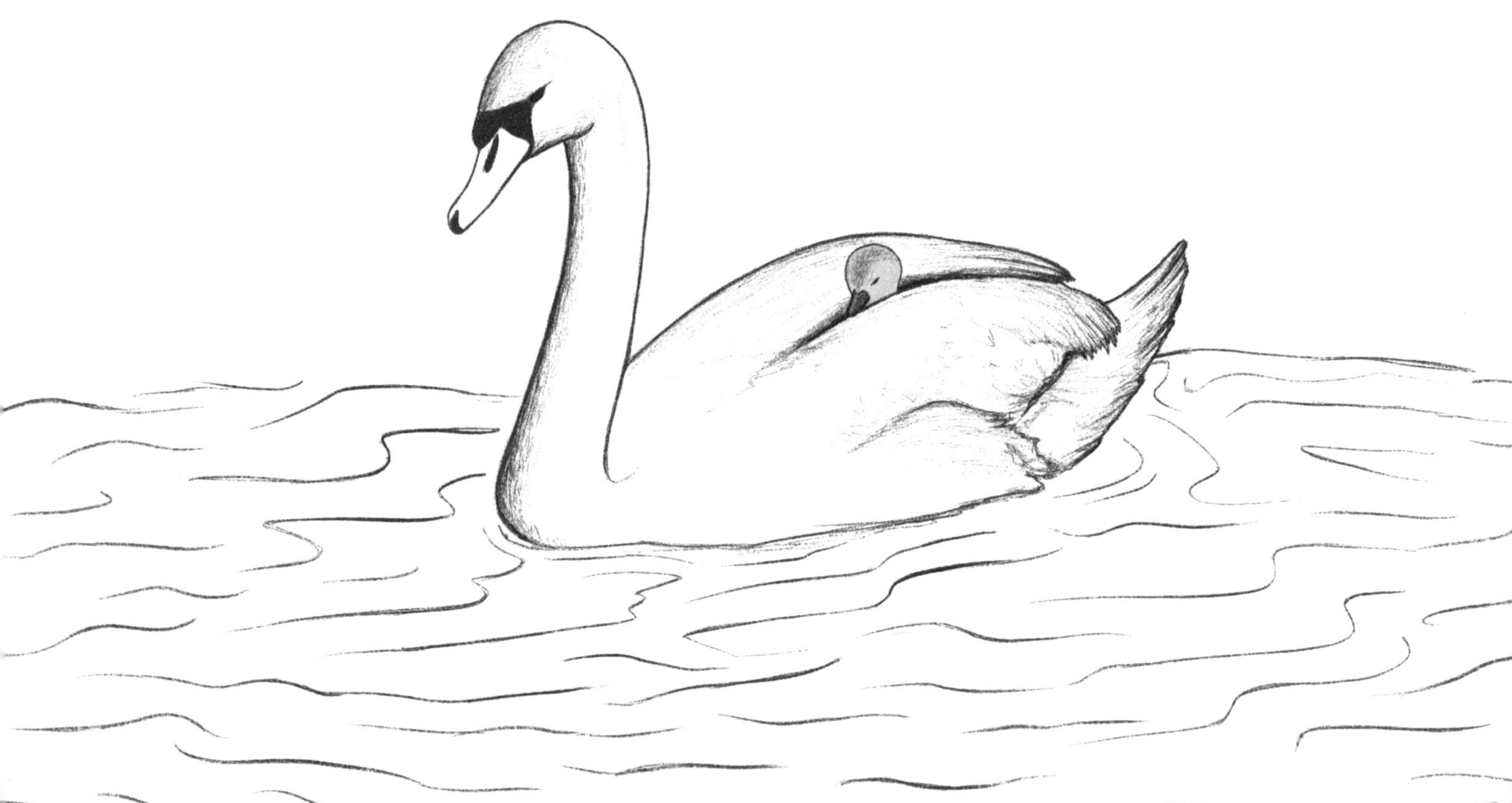

Don't ask for favors—

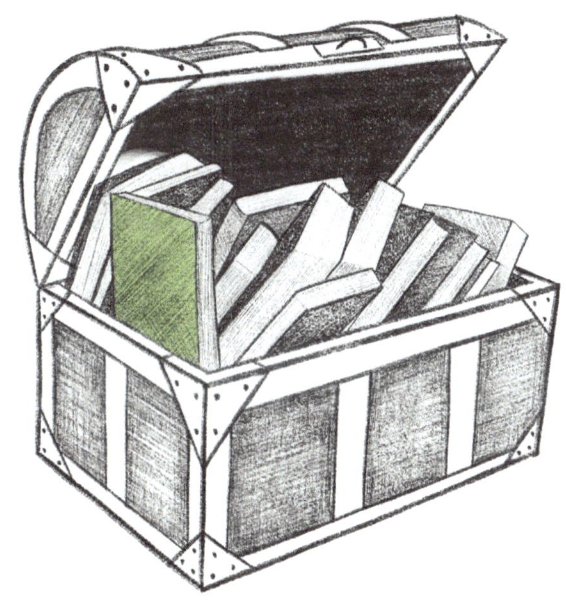

ask for advice.

We don't have control
over what we can control.

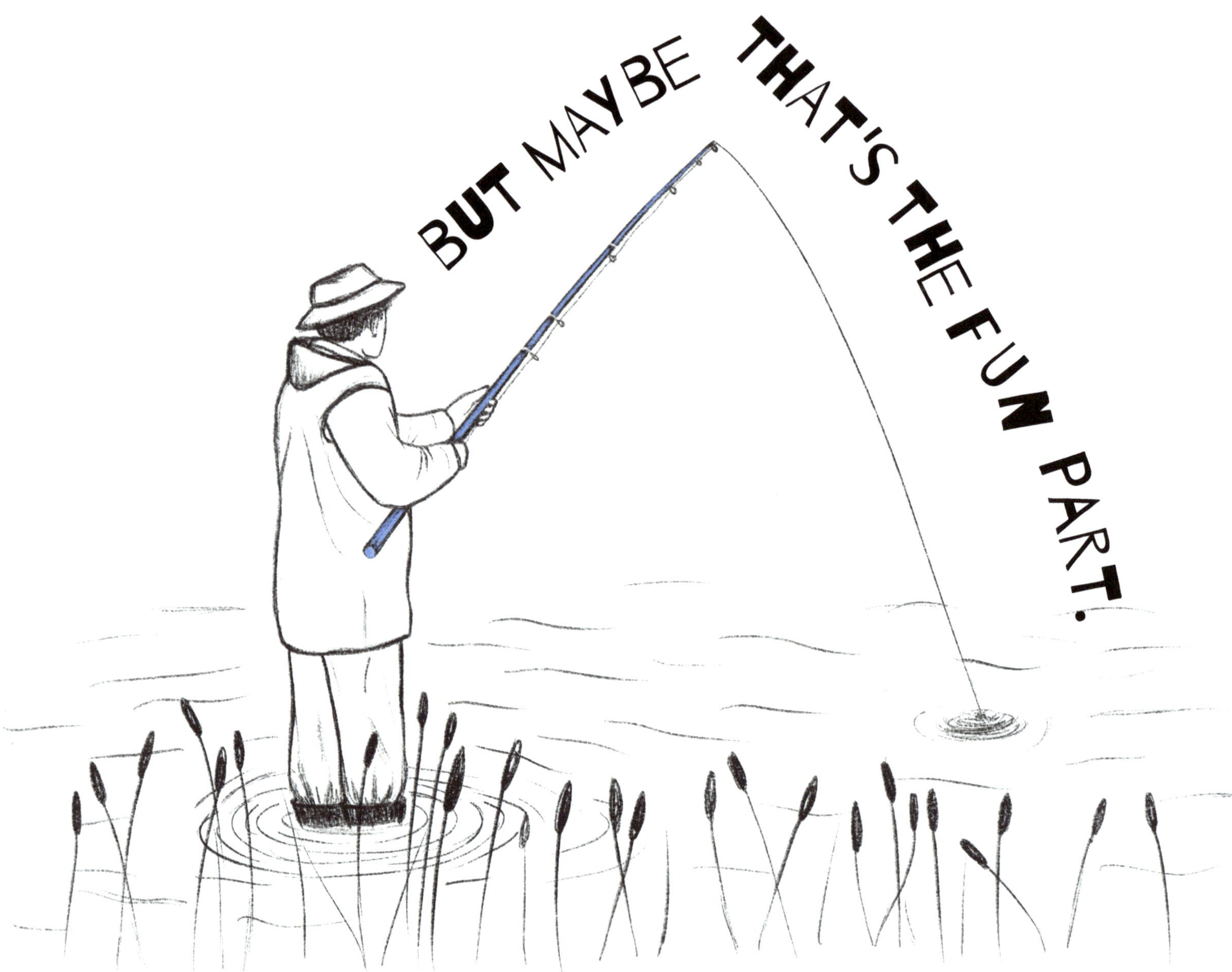

Not all signs are giant billboards.

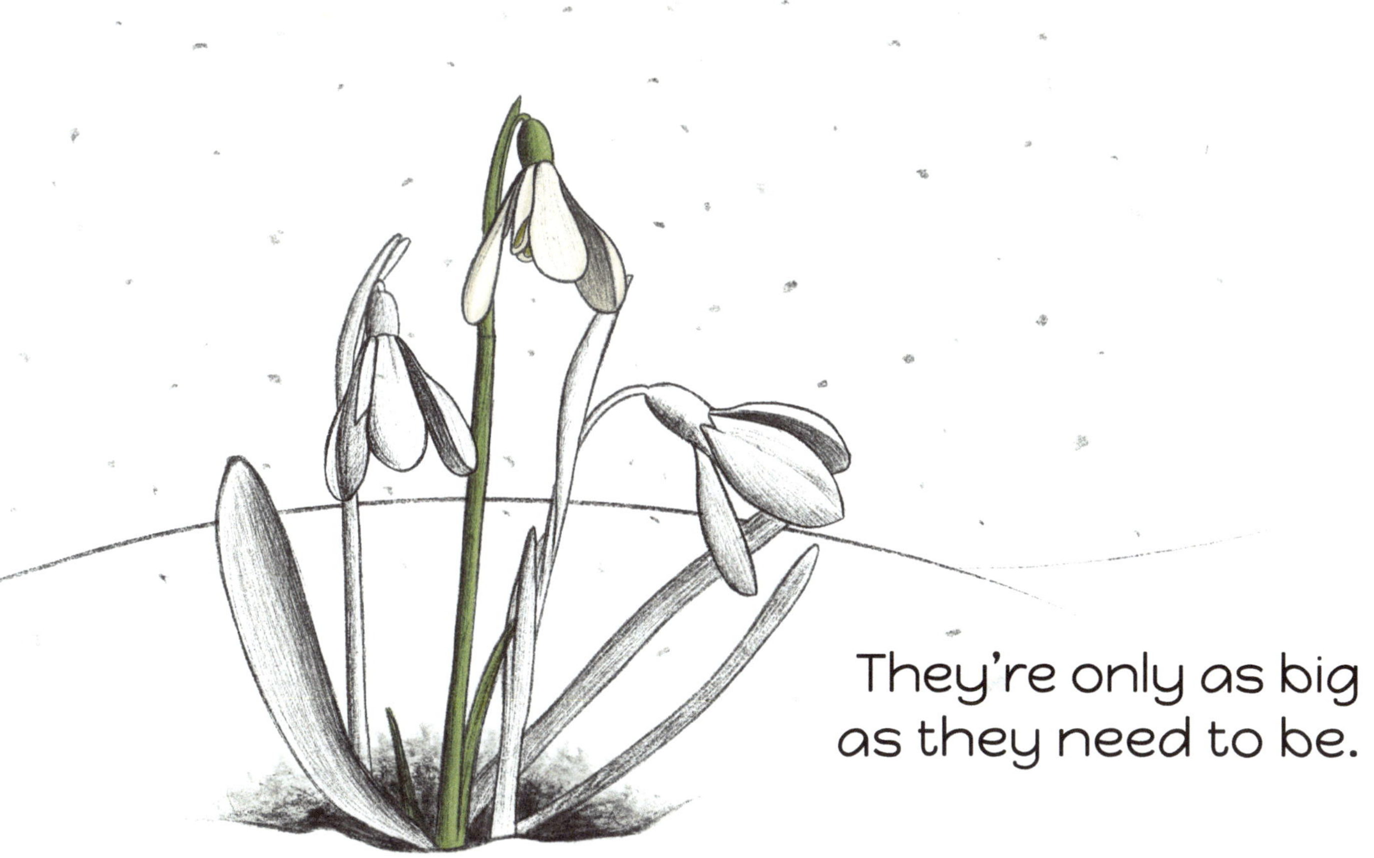

They're only as big
as they need to be.

The REWARD is
only worth the
SACRIFICE.

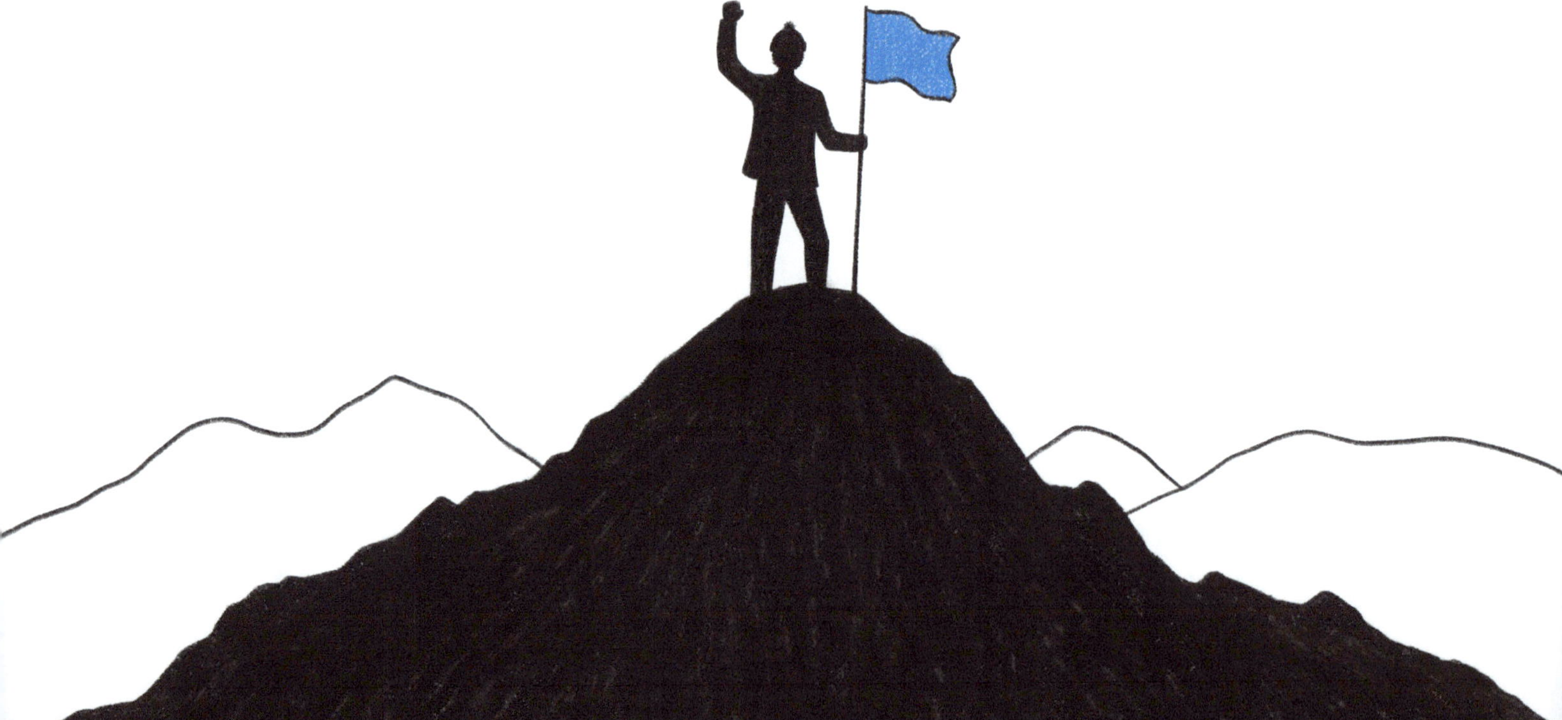

Never assume that anything is more important than the moment right now.

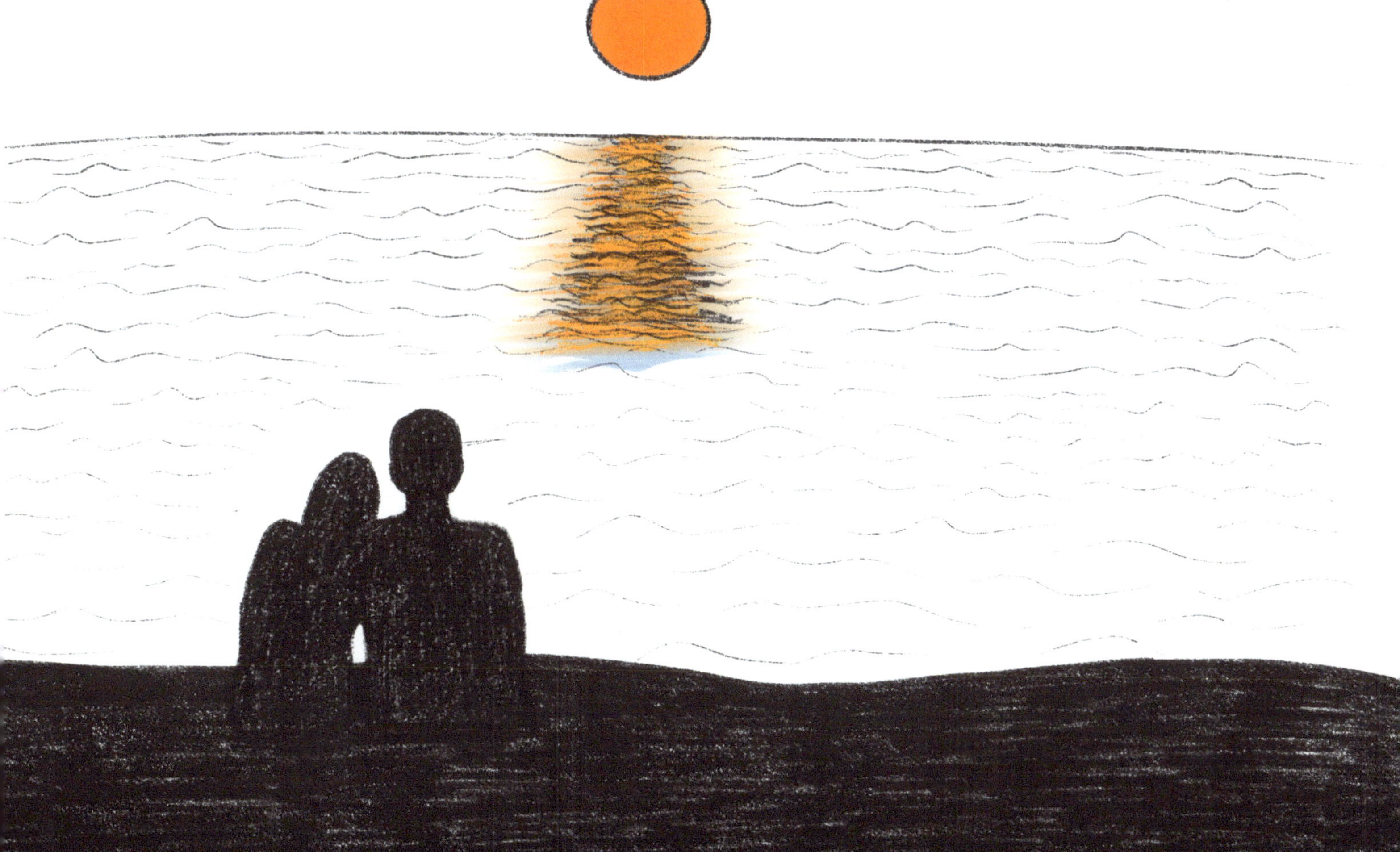

Flip a coin that's
compelled to answer.

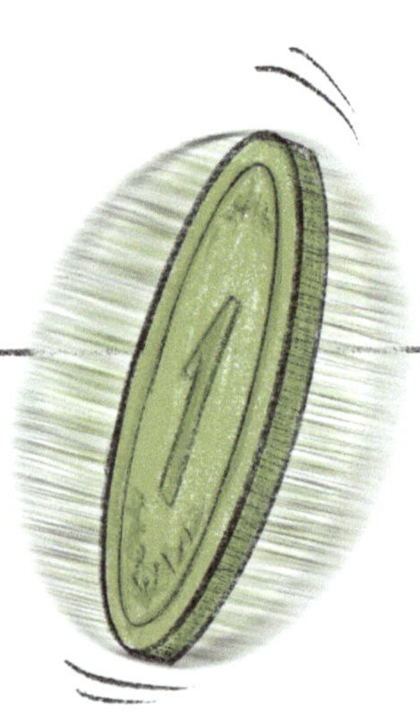

Then you will know.

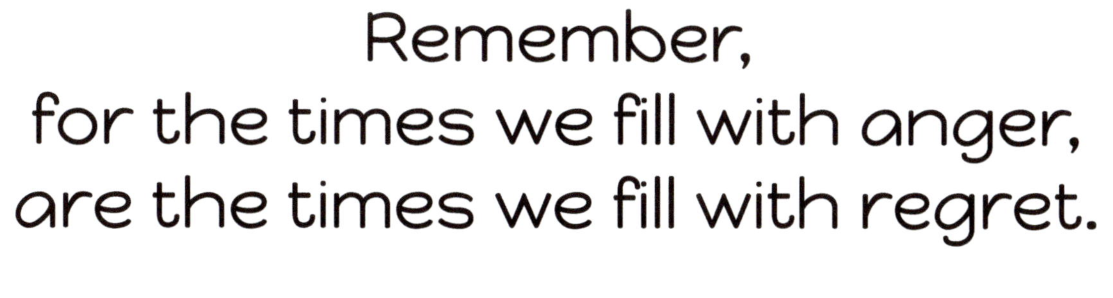

Remember,
for the times we fill with anger,
are the times we fill with regret.

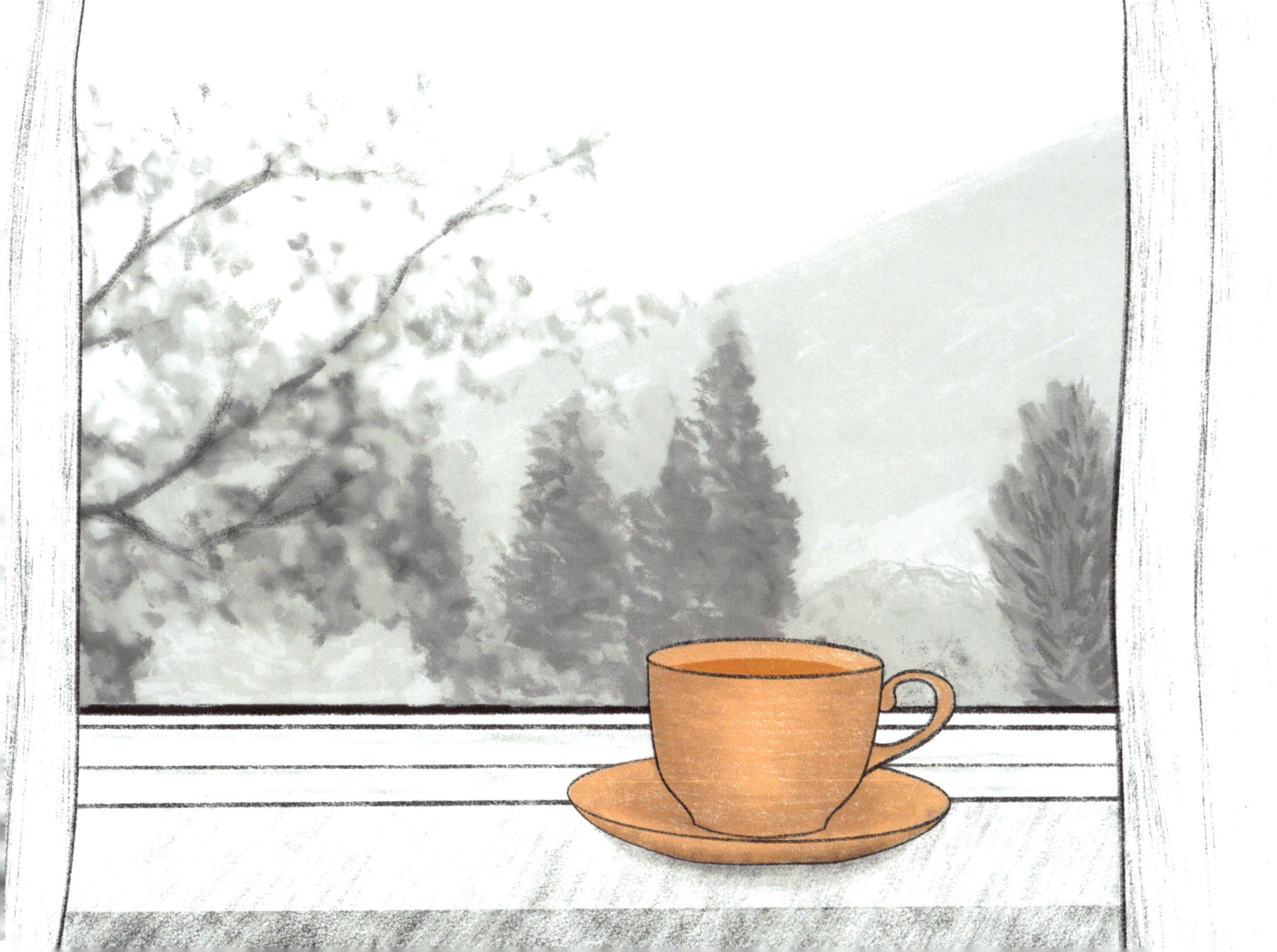

Success is a vocabulary—
you know all the words;
just pick the right ones
and put them in order.

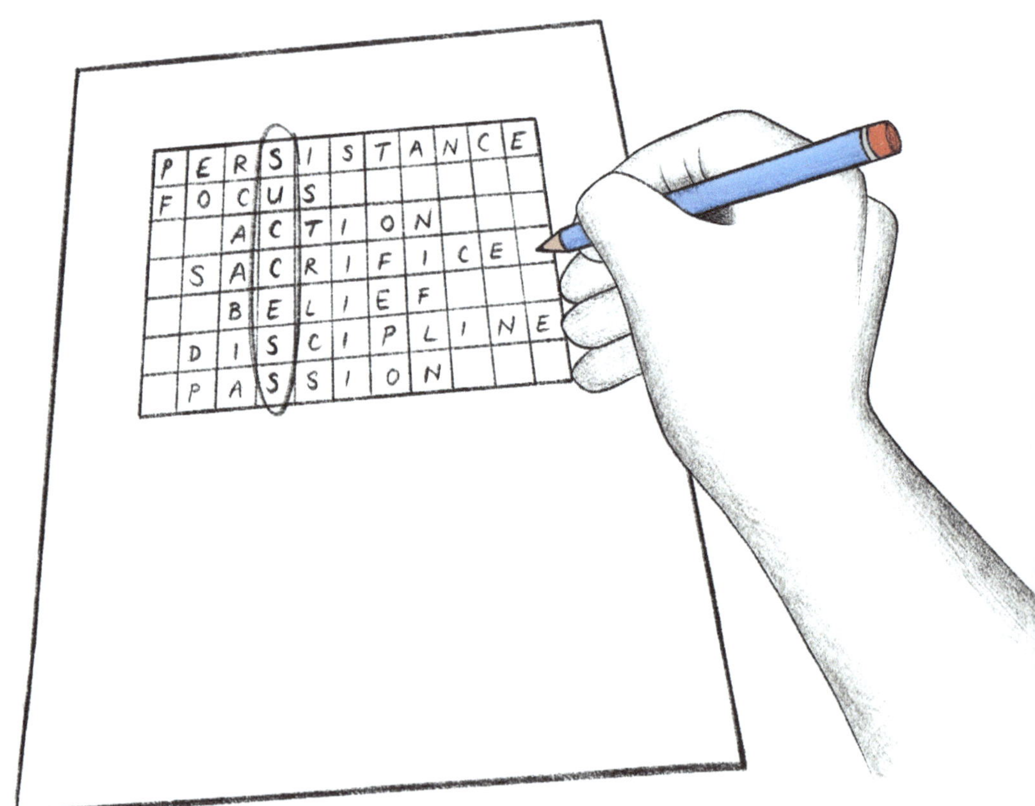

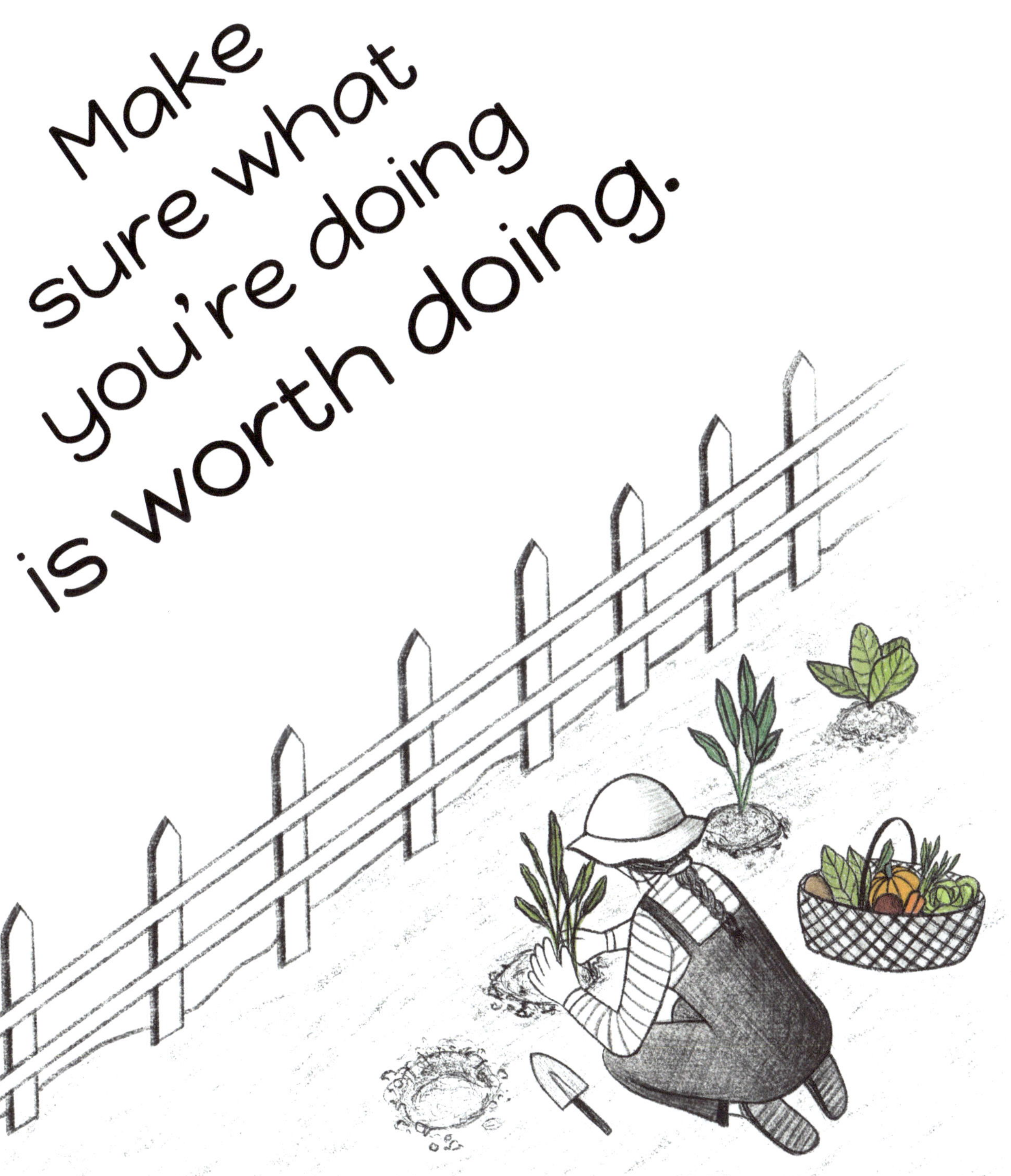

Make sure what you're doing is worth doing.

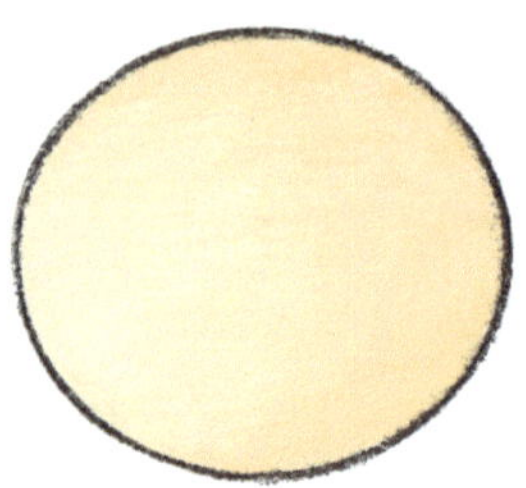

If there's always a tomorrow
we lose sight of today.
And today is what matters.
Until tomorrow.

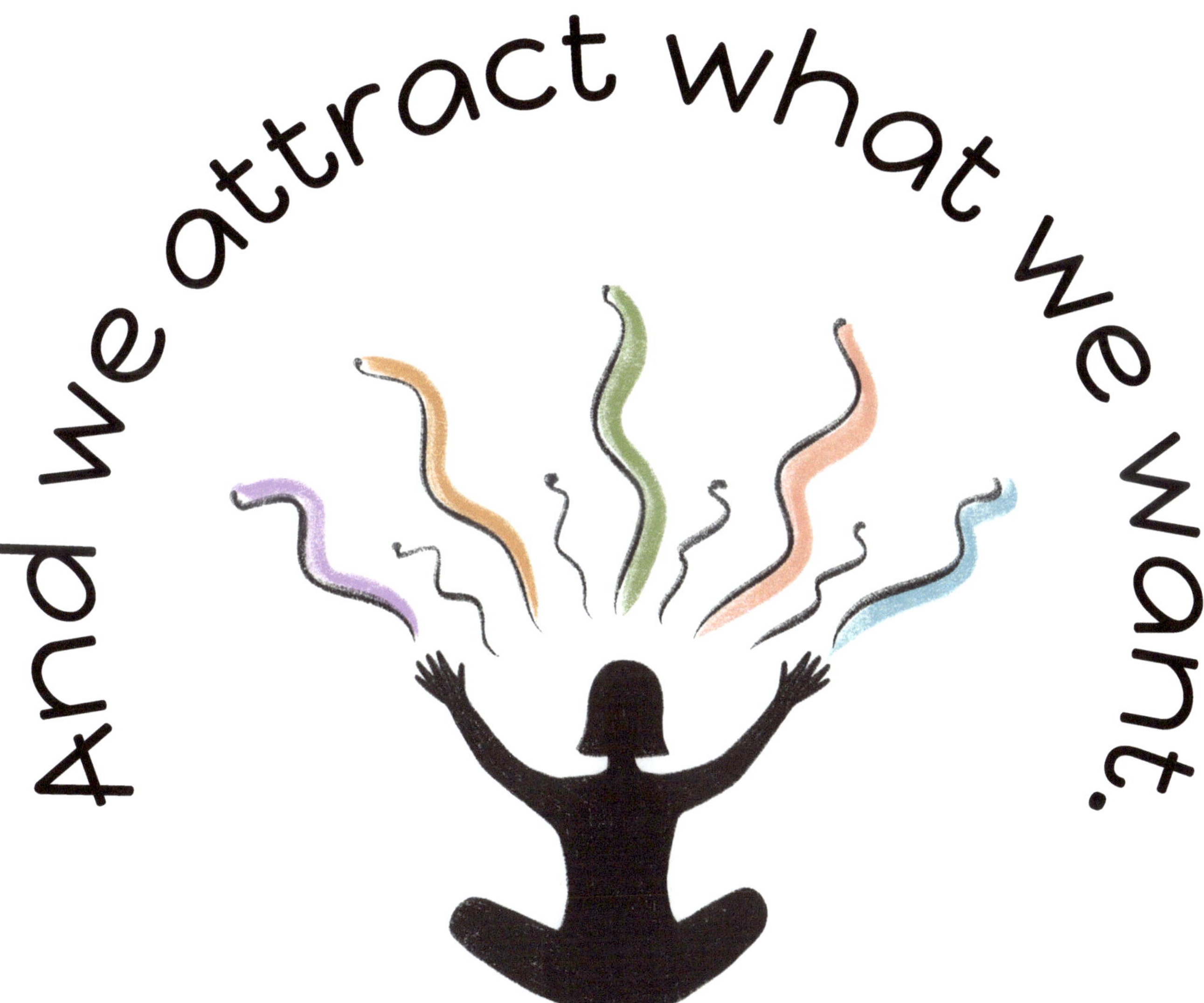

Life is as ___________ as you want it to be.
And we attract what we want.